CAN IT LIVE HERE?

By Jennifer B. Gillis

BARRON'S

Table of Contents

© Copyright 2006 by Barron's Educational Series, Inc.

All inquiries should be addressed to:
Barron's Educational Series, Inc.
250 Wireless Boulevard
Hauppauge, New York 11788
www.barronseduc.com

Library of Congress Catalog Card No.: 2005053588

ISBN-13: 978-0-7641-3291-9
ISBN-10: 0-7641-3291-1

Library of Congress Cataloging-in-Publication Data
Gillis, Jennifer Blizin, 1950–
    Can it live here? / Jennifer B. Gillis.
      p. cm. – (Reader's clubhouse)
    ISBN-13: 978-0-7641-3291-9
    ISBN-10: 0-7641-3291-1
    1. Animals—Habitations—Juvenile literature. I. Title. II. Series.

QL756.G55 2006
591.56'4—dc22

                                                          2005053588

PRINTED IN CHINA
9 8 7 6 5 4 3 2 1

Dear Parent and Educator,

Welcome to the Barron's Reader's Clubhouse, a series of books that provide a phonics approach to reading.

Phonics is the relationship between letters and sounds. It is a system that teaches children that letters have specific sounds. Level 1 books introduce the short-vowel sounds. Level 2 books progress to the long-vowel sounds. This progression matches how phonics is taught in many classrooms.

Can It Live Here? reviews the short-vowel sounds introduced in previous Level 1 books. Simple words with these short-vowel sounds are called **decodable words.** The child knows how to sound out these words because he or she has learned the sounds they include. This story also contains **high-frequency words.** These are common, everyday words that the child learns to read by sight. High-frequency words help ensure fluency and comprehension. **Challenging words** go a little beyond the reading level. The child will identify these words with help from the photograph on the page. All words are listed by their category on page 23.

Here are some coaching and prompting statements you can use to help a young reader read *Can It Live Here?*:

- **On page 4, "ant" is a decodable word. Point to the word and say:**

  Read this word. How did you know the word? What sounds did it make?

  Note: There are many opportunities to repeat the above instruction throughout the book.

- **On page 4, "lives" is a challenging word. Point to the word and say:**

  Read this word. It rhymes with "gives." How did you know the word? Did you look at the picture? How did it help?

You'll find more coaching ideas on the Reader's Clubhouse Web site: *www.barronsclubhouse.com.* Reader's Clubhouse is designed to teach and reinforce reading skills in a fun way. We hope you enjoy helping children discover their love of reading!

Sincerely,

Nancy Harris

Nancy Harris
Reading Consultant

An ant lives in an anthill.

Can it live in a shell?

A crab lives in a shell.

Can it live in a pen?

A ram lives in a pen.

Can it live in a den?

A fox lives in a den.

Can it live in a nest?

A robin lives in a nest.

Can it live in the sand?

A clam lives in wet sand.

Can it live on a plant?

A moth lives on a plant.

Can it live in a pond?

A frog lives in a pond.

Where do you live?

Fun Facts About Animal Homes

- Hermit crabs do not have their own shells. They move into empty shells that other animals have left behind.

- The giant white clam can be as large as 4 feet (1 m) across. That's about as wide as a teacher's school desk!

- Most crabs, foxes, and rats sleep during the day and are awake at night. They hunt for their food at night.

- Ants build many rooms inside their anthills. Some hold food, some are for raising young ants, and others are like ant bedrooms.

Find Out More

Read a Book

Ganeri, Anita. *Animal Homes.* Heinemann
Library, 2003.

Gregoire, Elizabeth. *Whose House Is This?:
A Look at Animal Homes—Webs, Nests,
and Shells.* Picture Window Books, 2005.

Visit a Web Site

Animal Homes

*http://kidport.com/RefLib/Science/
AnimalHomes.htm*

You can click on nine different animal
homes and get lots of good information
about each one. The site also gives you a
list of other books to read and other Web
sites you can visit for more information.

Glossary

 **anthill** a mound of mud or sand that covers the tunnels ants dig in the ground

 **clam** a sea animal with a one-hinged shell

 **hermit crab** a kind of crab that lives on land near the ocean and that people keep as pets

 **pen** a fenced-in area where farmers keep animals

 **ram** a male sheep

Word List

Challenging Words	anthill live lives	robin	
Decodable Short-Vowel Words	ant can clam crab den fox frog moth nest	pen plant pond ram sand shell wet	
High-Frequency Words	a an do in it the where you		

Index